Parables
of Jesus

by

B. A. Ramsbottom

2012
GOSPEL STANDARD TRUST PUBLICATIONS
12(b) Roundwood Lane
Harpenden, Herts
AL5 3BZ, England

D1161246

The Lost Sheep

The Lord Jesus often told interesting stories. We call them parables. They have a hidden meaning. They teach us about God and about ourselves. A parable is "an earthly story with a heavenly meaning".

Have you ever seen a flock of sheep grazing in the fields, or up in the hills? Perhaps there were a few little lambs frisking around. It is a lovely sight to see the sheep and their lambs.

Well, the Lord Jesus told the story of a shepherd who had a flock of a hundred sheep. He was a good, kind shepherd.

One day he found that one of his sheep was missing. It had wandered off, and was lost. (You know, sheep are foolish animals. They often wander away, and they can never find their way back.)

The shepherd, of course, was sad. He didn't forget the lost sheep because there were so many more. Nor did he say, "Well, it doesn't matter really! I have all these others."

What do you think he did? Carefully he made sure the others were all safe (ninety-nine of them!), and then he went off to search for the one that had strayed.

How long he was looking for it we do not know, nor how far he had to go. But we know the important thing. He found the sheep that had wandered away.

And what did he do when at last his sheep was found? Beat it? Shout at it? No, he was so happy. Lovingly, kindly he picked up the sheep, and carried it on his shoulders all the way back to the fold.

He was so pleased that he called his neighbours together and cried, "Rejoice with me for I have found my sheep which was lost."

Jesus Himself is the Good Shepherd. He loves His sheep so much that He died for them. And He goes after the wandering sheep till He finds it, and rejoices as He brings it back to the fold.

But aren't we like poor, wandering sheep? So ready to sin, so ready to go astray. We need the Lord Jesus to seek us and find us.

Here is a good prayer:

"Lord, the wandering sheep behold;
Bring him back into Thy fold;
On Thy shoulders bear him home;
Suffer him no more to roam."

You can read the story in Luke chapter 15, verses 3 to 7. It is usually called "The Parable of the Lost Sheep".

The Wicked Judge

There was once an important man. He was a judge. People who were being treated wrongly could come to him for help.

We still have judges today. They are usually good men. They see that the law is kept. They punish those who do wrong. They do not let people harm other people.

But this judge was wicked. Sadly he did not believe in God. Nor was he kind to other people. He did not want to help. He was a really bad man.

Now in the city where the judge lived there was a poor woman. She was a widow. She had no husband to help her. And someone was causing her a lot of trouble.

So she went and told the judge. She hoped he would help her. But no! He was unkind and did not want to help her at all.

So what do you think she did? She kept on going to the judge. She went again and again. In the end he was just weary and tired of her coming to him.

Now see a strange thing! He did not want to help her – but he thought, "I am weary and tired of her coming. She is a nuisance! She won't take no for an answer!"

So he helped her. He did everything she wanted – not because he liked her, nor because he was kind.

Just to get rid of her. So the poor woman got what she wanted.

Jesus told this parable to encourage us to pray. If this wicked man, who was so unkind, helped the poor woman at last, don't you think that God, who is kind and good, will help His children when they pray to Him?

Do you ever pray to God?

This story is usually called "The Parable of the Unjust Judge". You can read it in Luke chapter 18, verses 1 to 8.

road? He is different from the others. He does not belong to their country. He is a foreigner, a Samaritan.

Now the Jews and the Samaritans did not like one another. It must have been very disappointing for the poor wounded man that, of all people, it was a Samaritan who was coming.

But look! The Samaritan is going right up to him. When he sees him, he feels really sorry for him. Here is a friend at last!

Watch him doing everything he can to help the poor man. He pours oil and wine on his sores (just as we should use ointment). Then he bandages him up. But that is not the end!

Very tenderly the poor man is lifted up onto the Samaritan's donkey. Then he is taken to an inn, and carefully looked after. Don't you think all this was kind of the Samaritan? It is no wonder he is always called "the good Samaritan".

Soon the next day had arrived. We hope the wounded man was feeling better. His kind friend was still with him, but now he must go. What do you think was the last thing he did before he left? He paid the innkeeper for their stay, and told him still to look after his new friend till he was better. He himself would pay for everything.

It is a wonderful thing to have a good friend. But there is no friend like the Lord Jesus, the Son of God.

Like the good Samaritan He comes right where His people are, finds them in their sin and sorrow, and does everything for them. Nothing is too hard for Him, and His love is very great.

Do you know the little verse:

"Jesus, Friend of little children,
    Be a Friend to me;
Take my hand and ever keep me
    Close to Thee"?

This story is called "The Good Samaritan". You can read it in Luke chapter 10, verses 30 to 37.

The Wonderful Pearl

Have you ever seen a precious stone? Perhaps it has been a deep-red ruby, or a diamond sparkling in a ring.

In the days of Jesus it was the lovely white pearl that people specially thought of as precious.

Jesus once spoke about a man who was searching for these lovely pearls. He would give a lot of money for them. He tried to buy as many as he could.

But one day he saw a wonderful pearl. He had never seen one just like it before. It was so precious. It was so beautiful.

"Oh," he thought, "if only it were mine!"

He thought he would do anything if only he could have it for his very own. Perhaps you girls and boys sometimes have seen something and you have longed to have it for yourself.

But the man did not have enough money. He could not afford to buy it. So do you know what he did? He gathered together everything he had. Yes, even all the pearls he had already collected. And do you know what he did then? He sold the lot. He sold everything he had.

And then so happily he hurried to buy the wonderful pearl. He must have been so glad to have it at last. But there are not many people who want something so badly that they are willing to get rid of everything else, are there?

Jesus is just like that pearl – so precious. Many men and women, many girls and boys, have wanted Him so badly that they have felt they could give up everything else. You have all heard of Paul. He once said that he would gladly give up everything so that he might know the Lord Jesus for himself.

This parable is usually called "The Pearl of Great Price". You can read it in Matthew chapter 13, verses 45 and 46.

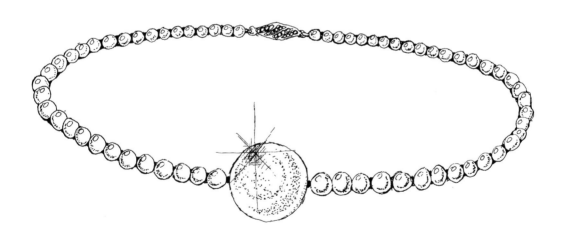

The Runaway Son

Two boys once lived together on a farm. They were brothers. They knew that one day everything would belong to them – the buildings, the land, the animals.

But the younger one could not wait. He was impatient. He wanted his share now. He longed to leave home and have a good time.

So he asked his father. He said, "Can I have my money now?" And his father said, "Yes" – though we think he must have felt very sad!

Very soon the son was off. He left home and went a long, long distance away. He took all his money with him.

Then he began to have a good time. He enjoyed himself. That is why he had left home. Some of the things he did were very sinful.

But soon all his money was gone. Now he was no longer happy.

But what had happened to all his friends? He had none – now that all his money was gone! They had all left him.

So he had to get a job. Do you know what it was? Looking after pigs. And he was so hungry that he would have been glad to eat the pigs' food (and that is not very nice!)

One day he began to think. He thought about the farm where he used to live. He thought about his father. Things were not so bad there, after all. At least he always had plenty to eat. Even the men who worked on the farm were well fed, and here he was, perishing with hunger.

Suddenly he spoke. "I am going back home! I shall tell my father how sorry I am, and how bad I have been. I know I am not good enough still to be his son, but I will ask him if I can be one of the workmen on the farm."

So up he got and set off on his long journey home. We do not know how long it took him. We know it was a long way, and if he had no money, he would have to walk, wouldn't he?

We wonder what he was thinking about as he journeyed. Was he wondering what his father would say to him? Would his father be angry? Would he speak to him?

But look! There is someone coming towards him. He is running. Why, it is his father! He has seen him, even when he was a long way off. See the father throwing his arms round his neck. Now he is kissing him. What a welcome!

"Father, I am sorry," says the runaway son. "I have done wrong. I am not good enough to be your son any more."

But his father is not listening. "Bring the best robe we have and put it on him." (His own clothes must have been very dirty – looking after pigs, and then the

long journey.) "Put a ring on his finger. Get some shoes for his feet." (He must have been barefooted.) "Let us have a feast and rejoice. This my son was dead, and he is alive again. He was lost, and is found."

Surely the poor son never, never expected such a welcome as this. His father couldn't rejoice enough! It was not only the son who was happy, but his father too.

Sadly the other brother was not happy. He was angry. He was not pleased to see his young brother. He grumbled to his father. He said, "I have never left home. I have always done my best. Why is there all this fuss about my brother?"

"No," said his father. "Everything I have is yours, my son. Don't be upset. Surely it is only right we should be glad and rejoice when your brother has come back home."

When sinners are brought to return to the Lord, confessing their sins, He is like the father in the story.

"Returning prodigals shall find
    Though they are base the Father's kind."

Those who come to Him in repentance and faith are lovingly received.

This story is usually called "The Prodigal Son". You can read it in Luke chapter 15, verses 11 to 32.

The Sower

One day a man went out into his field to sow seed. Slung over his neck was a bag holding the seed, and as he went he threw a handful here, and a handful there.

This was the old-fashioned way in which a field was sown with corn. (Perhaps you have seen the large machines that farmers use nowadays in springtime – ploughing up the ground and carefully dropping in the seed.)

What the farmer wants is the seed to grow, the corn to shoot up and then at last to have a good harvest. The corn will be reaped, then sold, and made into bread. And the farmer will be glad.

But a lot of the seed this man was sowing did no good at all.

Some of it, as he threw it, fell on the path. Immediately little birds came down and ate it up. They were glad to have a ready meal.

Some of the seed fell where there was not much soil. The ground was hard and rocky. But see! Surely the seed is growing well, and so quickly too. But no! The hot sun begins to beat down on the little shoot, and it withers away and dies.

Some of the seed fell among thorns and brambles. (You need to be careful you don't scratch yourself, don't you?) That seemed to do well. But as it grew, the thorns and the brambles grew too and choked the seed. So again the seed did no good.

Three places where the seed fell, and when harvest came – NOTHING.

But happily that is not the end. The farmer was not going to be disappointed. Some of the seed fell where the soil was good – not stony, not with lots of briars and brambles. And it began to grow, slowly at first. But when harvest time came there were lots of ears of good, ripe, golden corn. Some of the seed did better and brought forth more ears of corn than others, but all of it brought forth a good harvest.

How pleased the farmer must have been! Harvest time was always a time of great joy and gladness, and it was terrible if the harvest failed.

What does it all mean? Well, the Lord Jesus Himself explained. The seed is God's holy Word, the Bible. When the Word of God is preached, some people take no notice at all. Then others seem very pleased and interested, but it does not last. Others still seem even more interested and go on longer, but then they are more bothered about enjoying themselves or making money.

But there are always some who hear God's Word preached and are brought to know the Lord Jesus. Their hearts are opened by the Holy Spirit, God's Word enters, and their lives are truly changed.

How we need to pray that we might be like the

good ground! That what we hear about God, and sin, and heaven, and hell, and Jesus, might remain in our hearts and lives!

This story is usually called "The Parable of the Sower". You can read it in Matthew chapter 13, verses 3 to 8; 18 to 23; Mark chapter 4, verses 3 to 8; 14 to 20; and Luke chapter 8, verses 5 to 8; 11 to 15.

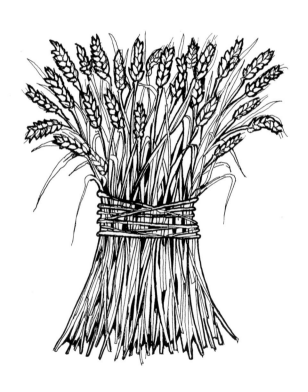

The Great Feast

There was once a man who had a beautiful meal made. It was a feast. The food must have been delicious (and plenty of it) for the Bible calls it "a great supper".

How lovely it must have been to be asked to that feast!

But see! A strange thing is happening. The man has sent a servant to go to all the guests and tell them that everything is ready. (They would already have been asked to go.)

But not one of them is going. Listen to what they are saying.

One says, "I have just bought some land. I am sorry I cannot come. I must go to see it."

How silly to buy some land without having seen it!

Another one says, "I have bought some oxen." (He would use them for ploughing.) "I must try them out. Please excuse me."

But, worst of all, one says that he has just got married. That means that he cannot come either. Why does he not bring his new wife with him?

Do you know what the real reason was why they did not come? They were not hungry.

Wasn't the man angry when his servant told him the news! What was to happen to all the beautiful food on the tables?

Well, he knew what he would do. It would not be wasted.

"Go as quickly as you can into the streets!" he said. "Tell the poor people there is a delicious feast and they are welcome to come – all sorts of people: those who are poor, or blind, or cripples."

Could these poor people really believe their ears? Was it really true? There was a feast, and they were asked to go! But how much would it cost? Nothing. How happy they must have been as they hurried there as fast as they could! You see, they were hungry; most of them would never have had a meal like this in their lives.

And still there was room! So the servant went out again until every table, every place was filled. "But make sure none of those who made excuses come in!" said the maker of the feast.

The good news about Jesus and His salvation is like a wonderful feast. But most people are not hungry, and so do not want to come. But there are always some who feel so unworthy, and yet long for these blessings. How glad they are to know they are welcome!

You can read this story in Luke chapter 14, verses 16 to 24. It is called "The Parable of the Great Supper".

The Two Houses

Have you ever watched a house being built? The bricks are laid in their place, the walls grow higher, the window frames and doors are put in, and at last the roof is put on.

But there is one part which you cannot see. It is underneath the house. We call it the foundation. It is what the house is built on and it must be hard, firm and solid.

Now watch these two houses going up. One is built so quickly and very soon is finished – almost before the other one is started. But look at the builder of the second house. He keeps digging, digging, digging. Why? He will not begin to build until he finds solid rock to build on.

At last the builder of the second house is happy. He has found solid rock. Now the building of his house can begin – on a firm foundation.

The other man has just not bothered. His house has no good foundation. It is just built on sand.

But why bother? There are the two lovely houses. What is the difference? Each is as comfortable as the other to live in. Surely the second builder did not need to take so much trouble, and spend so much time.

Then one day something happened. The sky grew dark. The rain began to fall. There was a dreadful storm. Have you ever looked through the window when a storm is raging? It is frightening, isn't it?

Well, not only was there this terrible storm but the wind blew hard and strong. It must have been almost like a gale. And then the water began to rise like a flood around the two houses.

Oh, but see the difference now! The one house, built on the rock, withstands the storm. There it stands, firm and unmoved. But, suddenly there is a crash, and the other house tumbles down in ruins. How sad for the builder!

It is not surprising that the Lord Jesus called one of the builders a foolish man, and the other a wise man. How silly not to bother about the important thing, the foundation! Why, the poor man has now lost all.

Everything except trusting in the Lord Jesus is like sinking sand. But those who trust in Jesus alone are like the man who built his house on the rock. They are safe.

You can read this story in Matthew chapter 7, verses 24 to 27 and in Luke chapter 6, verses 46 to 49. It is sometimes called "The House on the Sand, and the House on the Rock".

The Middle of the Night

Jesus once asked a question: He said, "What do you think would happen?" – and then went on:

Suppose it was very late one night. There was a knock at your door. A friend had called to see you – but you did not know he was coming. It was a complete surprise. And, oh dear! you had nothing to give him to eat.

Just think of it: a friend come to see you, and you haven't even a loaf of bread! What can you do?

So, though it is dark and late, you go out. You can't leave your friend with nothing to eat, so you must get something. You go to another friend's house to tell him what has happened.

But it is now the middle of the night. And your friend is in bed! His children are in bed too. He doesn't like being knocked up in the middle of the night. Have you ever been fast asleep, and suddenly someone has woken you up, asking for something?

So what does he say? "Please don't bother me at this time of night." But you do not go away. You want to borrow some bread. And you won't go away without it. You would be ashamed to go back and not have anything for your visitor to eat.

Now then, says Jesus, the man in bed may not want to get up. He may not even want to help his friend. But because he keeps standing there, and

won't go away, in the end he does get up and gives him everything he wants.

Now this is Jesus' question. Do you think God will answer His people's prayers? Do you think, when they keep calling on Him, He will refuse to answer? Do you think it will be too much trouble for Him?

"No," says Jesus, "ask, and it shall be given you. Seek, and ye shall find. Knock, and it shall be opened to you."

Do you know the little verse:

"Thou art coming to a King,
　　Large petitions with thee bring;
For His grace and power are such,
　　None can ever ask too much"?

And nothing is too hard for Him. He is almighty. He says, "I am the Lord, the God of all flesh: is there anything too hard for Me?"

You can read this story in Luke chapter 11, verses 5 to 10. It is usually called "The Parable of the Friend at Midnight".

Not Ready!

Some of you may have been to a wedding. Perhaps you have even been a bridesmaid? or a page boy?

In Bible days weddings were usually at night. It seems strange to us, doesn't it? Late at night the man being married went with his friends to the home of his bride and took her back to his own home. Others waited for the procession, and then joined it.

Now in the story Jesus told there were ten girls waiting for the man who was to be married (the bridegroom) to come. Of course, because it was dark, they had to take lamps with them, lamps that were lit by oil.

But this night they did have to wait a long time. They waited and waited. Why was the bridegroom not coming? So tired were they that they all fell asleep!

Suddenly they woke up. What was happening? Someone was shouting that the bridegroom had come. Why (can it be possible?), it is midnight. They must have been asleep a long time.

They all jumped up – but five of the girls were in darkness. Their lamps had gone out while they were sleeping. They had been very foolish indeed. They had not bothered to bring any oil with them to keep their lamps burning.

Immediately they turned to the others, whose

lamps were still alight. "Give us some of your oil," they begged. "Our lamps have gone out."

"No!" said the others. They were not being selfish but they needed all their oil to keep their own lamps burning. "Go quickly and buy some!" they said.

So the five girls who had been so silly as not to bring oil for their lamps went off to see if they could buy some.

But now see! The bridegroom is here. All are going with him. The five girls with their lamps burning brightly join the procession. Now they are arriving at the house. They all go in for the wedding feast. "And the door was shut."

O, but what has happened to the other girls? Where are they? They have not arrived back yet.

Now see them coming. They are knocking at the door. But, sadly, it is too late. They are calling for the door to be opened, but they are not allowed to go in.

This is one of the saddest stories Jesus told. He ended it by saying, "Watch therefore, for ye know neither the day nor the hour wherein the Son of man cometh." One day Jesus will come in great glory. The thing that matters is to be ready, to be prepared for when Jesus comes.

Five of the ten girls were ready; the other five were not. Five went in; the other five were shut out. For ever!

Are you and I ready for when Jesus comes? Do you ever pray:

"Prepare me, gracious God,
　　To stand before Thy face,
Thy Spirit must the work perform,
　　For it is all of grace.

"In Christ's obedience clothe,
　　And wash me in His blood;
So shall I lift my head with joy,
　　Among the sons of God"?

This story is usually called "The Parable of the Ten Virgins", or "The Parable of the Wise and Foolish Virgins". You can read it in Matthew chapter 25, verses 1 to 13.

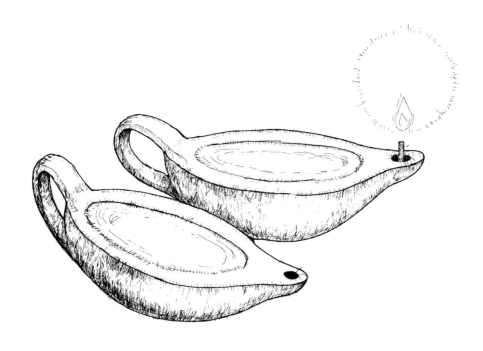